ᓖᑎᐊᑉ
ᓯᐊᕐᕋᔭᐅᑎᑐᐊᓇᖓ
LIITIA'S ONE-SKI

ᑎᑎᕋᖅᑐᖅ
ᔭᕗᕆ ᑯᕋᒃ ᐊᒻᒪ
ᑲᐃᓚᓐ ᒪᐃᕋᓐ

ᑎᑎᖅᑐᒐᖅᑐᖅ
ᐃᒪ ᐲᑐᓴᓐ

WRITTEN BY
Jeffrey Kheraj and
Kahlan Miron

ILLUSTRATED BY
Emma Pedersen

ᓖᑎᐊ ᖃᐅᓱᐃᑦᑐᒥᐅᑕᖅ, ᓄᓇᕗᒻᒥ. ᐅᑭᐅᑉ ᐃᓛᖕᒐᓂ, ᐊᓈᓇᑦᓯᐊᒃᑯᒥᓐᓄᑦ ᓂᕆᖃᑖᖅᑐᖅ. ᑐᓵᑎᓐᓇᓱᒡᒧ ᐊᓈᓇᑦᓯᐊᓂ ᐅᓂᒃᑳᑦᓚᒍ ᓱᕈᓯᐅᓯᓂᕆᒥᓂᒃ. ᓖᑎᐊ ᐊᓈᓇᑦᓯᐊᖕᓗ ᐃᑐᐊᕐᒪᑦ ᐊᐱᓯᓚᓂᒃ ᐱᖕᓯᓂᒃ ᑕᑯᖕᒃ. "ᐅᓪᓗᒥ ᑎᓯᕐᕕᑦᒧ ᓈᒻᒪᑎᐊᖅᐳᖅ," ᐊᓈᓇᑦᓯᐊᒻᒪ ᐅᖃᖅᑐᓂ. ᓖᑎᐊ ᐊᖕᑎᖅᑐᖅ.

Liitia lives in Qausuittuq (Resolute Bay), Nunavut. One spring day, she visits her grandma for lunch. She loves hearing her grandma's stories about when she was a child.

Liitia and her grandma look out the window at the snow-covered hills.

"Today is a perfect day for sliding," says Grandma. Liitia agrees.

ᐊᓈᓇᑦᓯᐊᒐ ᐅᖃᖅᐳᖅ, "ᓂᕕᐊᖅᓯᐊᕐᔪᑎᓪᓗᒐ, ᑎᓯᕋᐊᖅᐸᓚᐅᖅᑐᒍᑦ ᐅᐱᕐᖔᒥᖅ. ᑎᓯᐅᑎᖅᖅᐸᓚᐅᙱᑦᑐᒍᖦᑕ ᐅᓪᓗᒥ ᓱᕈᓯᕐᓄᑦ ᐊᑐᖅᑕᐅᔪᖅᑐᓂᒃ. ᖅᐳᓯᓐᓇᑦ ᑎᓯᕋᖅᐸᓚᐅᖅᑐᒍᑦ!"

Grandma says, "When I was a girl, we would go sliding all spring long. But we didn't use the sleds kids use today. We would slide on sealskins!"

ᓖᑎᐊᑉ ᑭᓇᑯᓗᐊ ᖁᕕᐊᐊᑐᖅ. ᐋᓇᓇᑦᓯᐊᖓ ᐅᓂᒃᑳᖃᓂᑦᓴᓂ
ᓄᓇᓕᖕᓂ ᓱᕈᓯᓕᒫᑦ ᓴᒡᕋᖅᑕᐅᑎᓇᓱᖃᑦᑕᐅᑎᖓᓂᖓᓂᒃ. ᐋᓇᓇᑦᓯᐊᖓ
ᓯᕗᓪᓕᖅᐹᑎᐊᕗᔪᖃᓪᓚᕆᒃ. ᓴᒡᑲᒻᒪᑎᐅᖅᓯᒪᕐᒧᓗᓂ ᐃᓐᓇᓂᒃ!

Liitia's face lights up. Grandma goes on to tell her about how all the kids in the community competed. Grandma was always the fastest. She even won against some adults!

ᐅᒃᔪᒥᑦᑖᕋᓗᐊᕐᒪᑕ, ᓖᑎᐊ ᐃᓕᓐᓂᐊᕐᕕᖕᒧᑦ ᐱᓱᑎᓪᓗᓂ. ᐊᖅᑯᓵᖅᓯᒪᒥ ᐱᖕᒍᖅᓯᐊᒎᕐᒥ ᑕᑯᓪᓗᓂ ᓯᑐᓯᓂᒃ ᐊᖕᒐᔭᑎᓂᒃ ᑎᓯᕐᖅᑐᓂᒃ.

After lunch, Liitia walks back to school. She passes a big hill and sees some older kids sliding on it.

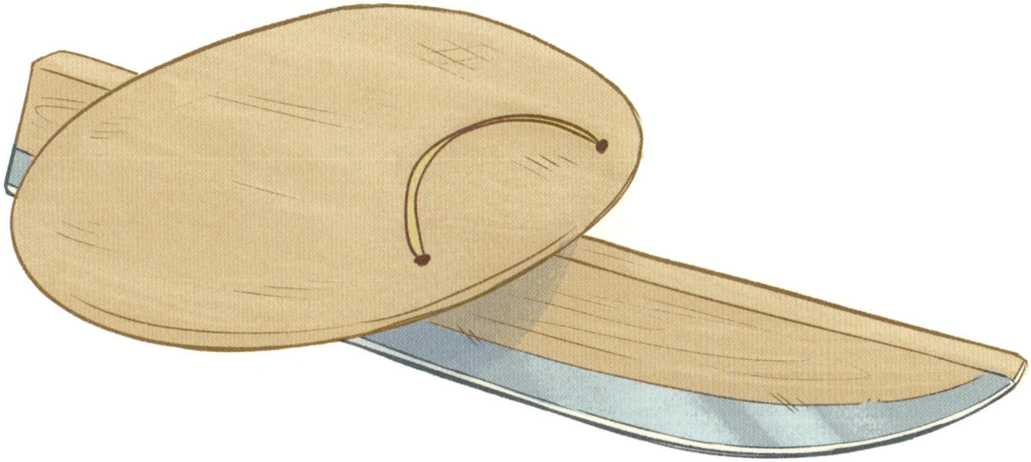

ᓱᕈᓯᖅ ᐱᖒᑉ ᖄᖕᒪᓃᑦᑐᖅ ᓯᕗᒧᒥᐊᕋᒥ ᑎᓯᓚᖅᑐᓂ. ᓯᐊᕐᕆᔭᐅᑎᑐᐊᓚᖕᒥᒃ ᐊᑐᖅᑐᖅ. ᓯᐊᕐᕆᔭᐅᑎᑐᐊᓚᒃ ᑎᓯᕋᐅᑎ ᐃᒃᓯᕙᐅᑕᖄᕐᔪᑐᐃᓐᓇᖅᑐᓂ ᓯᐊᕐᕆᔭᐅᑎᑐᐊᖃᖅᑐᓂ. ᓱᒃᑲᓚᔪᐊᓘᓪᓗᓂ.

ᑎᓱᔭᓈᕐᒥ, ᐱᖃᓐᓇᕆᔭᖕᒥᓐᓄᑦ ᐊᒡᒐᖕᒥᑦ ᐸᑎᒃᑕᐅᕗᑦ. “ᐱᒃᑯᓇᖅᑐᐊᓘᑲᐃᓐᓇᖅᑐᖅ!” ᐱᖃᑎᖓ ᐅᖃᖅᐳᖅ. “ᓵᓚᖃᓪᓚᑦᑖᓛᖅᑐᑎᑦ ᓵᓚᖃᕋᓱᒃᑐᖃᓚᖅᐸᑦ!”

A kid at the top of the hill pushes off and starts sliding down. He's sliding on a one-ski. A one-ski is a sled with a small seat and one runner that slides like a ski. He goes very fast.

When he reaches the bottom, his friends high-five him. "Nice one!" his friend says. "You'll definitely win at the competition!"

ᓖᑎᐊᑉ ᓯᑐᔨᑦ ᐅᑉᐸᑦᑐᓂᒃ. "ᖃᖓ ᓱᓕᖃᕐᑲᑕᖃᓛᕐᒪᑦ?" ᐊᐱᕆᕗᖅ.

"ᑎᑭᑦᓴᓕᐅᑉ ᓄᖕᒍᐊᓂ," ᐅᖃᖅᐳᖅ ᕼᐊᓐᑐᑦ, ᐱᔾᑲᑯᑦ ᐊᒎᐊᑕᖅᑐᖅ. "ᐊᔾᓯᒌᖕᒥᑦᑐᓂᒃ ᓯᒃᑲᐅᑎᓕᖅᑐᑦ, ᐃᓄᐃᓗ ᓱᓕᖃᐅᓯᐊᖅᑕᖅᑐᑎᒃ. ᐆᑦᑐᕆᐊᑦ?"

Liitia goes up to the kids. "When is the competition?" she asks.

"It's at the end of the season," says Hunter, the boy who went down the hill. "There are different kinds of races, and people compete for prizes. You wanna try?"

ᓖᑎᐊᑉ ᓯᖕᖓᕐᔭᕐᑐᓂ ᑕᑯᕙ ᓯᐊᕐᓯᐅᑎᑐᐊᕐᒥᑦ. ᑕᒪᐃᐦᑐᒥᒃ ᐃᑭᒪᑕᕐᖃᔭᓛᕐᒻᒪᑕ.
"ᐋ, ᖁᔭᓐᓇᒥᒃ, ᐃᓚᓐᓂᐊᕐᕕᐊᑎᐊᕐᖃᑕᕋᒪ," ᐅᖃᖅᑐᓂ, ᑐᐊᕝᕕᐊᓪᓚᒃᐳᖅ.

Liitia looks at the one-ski nervously. She has never ridden one before. "Oh, thanks, but I have to get back to school," she says, rushing off.

ᓖᑎᐊ ᐊᖏᕐᕋᕋᒥ, ᐊᖓᔪᖅᑳᓂ ᐅᖃᐅᑎᕙ ᓵᓚᖃᕋᓱᖅᑐᓂᒃ
ᑕᐅᖅᑲᐅᓂᕐᒥᓪᓗ ᓯᒡᔭᓂᒃ ᓯᐊᕐᓯᔭᐅᑎᑐᐊᓕᕐᓂᒃ.

When Liitia gets home, she tells her parents about the competition and seeing the kids racing one-skis.

ᐊᑖᑕᖓ ᐅᖃᖅᐳᖅ, "ᓯᐊᕐᓯᔪᐅᑎᐊᓗᖃᖅᑲᖅᑐᖓ ᓯᔾᔭᐃᒥ. ᑭᓯᐊᓂ, ᓴᓇᑕᐊᖃᖕᓂᐊᕋᒃ. ᐊᕐᕋᒍᓕᕋᖕᒎᓂ ᑕᐃᑲᓃᒪᓕᑦ."

ᓘᑎᐊ ᖁᕕᐊᕐᑕᕐᑐᓂ. "ᕼᐃᒻᒪᑦᑕᖅ?" ᐅᖃᖅᐳᖅ ᖁᕕᐊᕐᑕᕐᑐᓂ. "ᑕᑯᕙᖕᓇᖅᐸᐅ?"

Her dad says, "I have an old one-ski in the shed. It needs some work, though. It's been out there for years."

Liitia perks up. "Really?" she asks excitedly. "Can I see it?"

ᐅᖁᒪᐃᑦᑎᑦᓯᖕᒪᑕ, ᓲᑎᐊᒃ ᐊᓈᓇᖕᒧᑦ ᑕᑯᑎᑕᖅᑐᖅᐳᒃ ᓯᐊᕐᕆᔭᐅᑎᒍᐊᓕᖕᒥ.

ᓯᓕᕗᖅ ᐃᓄᐊ, ᓯᐊᕐᕆᔭᐅᑎᒍᐊᒃ ᐱᑐᖅᑲᒎᖅ. ᓯᐊᕐᕆᔭᐅᑎᖕᓐ ᒪᖕᒋᖅᑐᓕᐅᑎᓐᓯᓇ ᐃᒃᓯᕙᐅᑕ ᓄᑎᖅᓯᓕᓐᓯᓇ. ᐊᒃᑐᓇᓯᖕᓐ ᕿᑐᖅᓯᓕᓐᓯᓇ. ᓲᑎᐊ ᖃᓄᐃᖕᓴᓯᓂ. ᖃᑯᐊᒐᑦᑕ ᓯᐊᕐᕆᔭᐅᑎᒍᐊᖃᕐᒥ. ᐱᓕᒻᒥᒃᓴᖃᑦᑕᖅᐸᑦ, ᓴᓐᓇᕈᒃᑐᓂᖃᑕᐅᕐᖓᓂᐊᖅᑐᒃᓴᐅᕐᖅ!

After dinner, Liitia's dad takes her out to show her the one-ski.

He was right, the one-ski is old. It has a rusty runner and a cracked seat. The rope handle is broken. But Liitia doesn't care. She is just excited to have a one-ski. If she practises, maybe she can be in the competition!

ᖃᐅᑦᑐᒍ ᐃᓕᓐᓂᐊᕐᕕᖕᒥ, ᓖᑎᐊᒃ ᓴᖅᑭᑦᑎᓂᐅᒃ ᓯᐊᕐᓯᔭᐅᑎᔭᓕᖕᓂ ᒪᖕᒋᖅᑐᓯᔪᕐᔭᖅ. ᓯᓗᑦᓕᒥ ᐱᖕᒍᕋᑦᒃᑯᑦ ᐆᑐᖅᑐᓂᐅᒃ. ᓯᓗᑦᓯᖃᕐᒥ ᑎᓯᓪᓯᒥ, ᓯᒃᓯᓗᐊᕋᓂ. ᓖᑎᐊ ᐃᒃᓯᕚᐅᑕᖕᓗᔪᖕᓇᑎᕚᓂ. ᓴᖕᒍᕌᕐᒥ, ᐃᔾᑲᖅᑐᓂ ᓯᐊᕐᓯᔭᐅᑎᔭᓕᖕᒥᓂᑦ.

The next day after school, Liitia takes out her rusty old one-ski. She tries it on a small hill at first. On her first run, she isn't very good. Liitia can barely stay in her seat. When she tries to turn, she falls off her one-ski.

ᓖᑎᐊ ᓴᐱᓕᕐᕕᓐ. ᐅᒃᑑᖃᐅᓂᖅᑐᓂ ᐅᐋᓂᑕᓕᕐ, ᑲᑕᒃᐸᒃᑐᓂ, ᐱᒃᓯᒃᐸᒃᑐᓂᓗ.

But Liitia doesn't give up. She tries again after every wobble, fall, and crash.

ᓕᑦᐊ ᐃᓕᓐᓂᐊᕐᕕᖕᒥᑦ ᐱᓕᒻᒪᒃᓴᐃᓐᓇᖅᑐᓂ. ᑕᐃᒫᒃᑕᒐ ᐱᔪᓐᓇᖅᓯᐊᑐᖅᑐᓂ. ᓄᖅᑲᖕᓇᖅᓯᕐᓱᓂ, ᓴᖑᕙᓐᓇᖅᓯᕐᓱᓂ, ᐳᒃᑲᓗᒐᓐᓇᖅᓯᕐᓱᓂᔾᔪᐃᑦ ᓯᐊᕐᓯᐳᑎᐊᑕᖕᒥᓄᑦ.

ᓕᑦᐊ ᖃᐅᔨᒪᓪᓗᓂ ᓴᓕᖃᕐᑐᖕᓂᖃᑕᐅᓂᐊᕈᓂ, ᓯᒃᑕᓂᑭᓴᐅᑎᓇᕐᓯᐊᕐᓃᓇᑕᐊᖅᑰᓂᕐᒥᒃ.

ᐅᓪᓗᐃᑦ ᐃᓚᖕᒥᓂ ᓕᑦᐊᕝ ᓴᐊᓐᑐᕐ ᑕᑰᓪᓗᓂᐅᒃ ᐃᓕᓐᓂᐊᖕᓯᖅᑎᓪᓗᒋᑦ. ᐊᐱᕆᓪᓗᓂᐅᒃ ᓯᒃᑕᓂᑭᓴᐅᑎᕈᒪᒪᖕᒌᑦ.

ᓴᐊᓐᑐᕐ ᖁᖕᒡᓗᑐᓂ. "ᐊᐱᕐᓯᓚᒃ!" ᐅᖃᖅᑐᓂ.

Liitia keeps practising after school. Eventually she gets better. She can stop, turn, and even make small jumps on her one-ski.

But Liitia knows that if she wants to be in the competition, she needs to practise racing.

One day Liitia finds Hunter after school. She asks him if he wants to race.

Hunter smiles. "You're on!" he says.

ᓖᑎᐊ ᖁᕕᐊᑦᑕᑐᓂ. ᐱᖕᒐᔪᐊᒥ, ᓱᖕᒐᓚᑦᑕᖅᑐᓂ. ᕼᐊᐣᑐᕐ ᓯᒃᓴᒃᓴᔪᓪᓕ.
ᓯᐊᕐᓯᔭᐅᑎᒍᐊᓚᐦᓗ ᐱᐅᓂᖅᖄᓗᒐᓗᓂ ᐱᖕᓚᓂᑦ.
ᐱᓕᐊᑦᐊᓇᑕᖃᑕᖅᓱᑎᒃ. ᕼᐊᐣᑐᕐ ᓇᓴᐃᑕᖅᑐᓂ.
"ᐱᖕᓘᓪ...ᒪᕐᕉᒃ...ᐊᑕᐅᓯᖅ, ᐊᓖ!" ᕼᐊᐣᑐᕐ ᐅᖃᖅᑐᓂ.
ᓯᒃᓴᐅᑎᓪᓗᑎᒃ ᐱᖕᒍᒃᑯᑦ. ᓖᑎᐊ ᓯᒃᑕᕐᕕᖕᕙᒐᓪᓱᓂ ᓇᓴᐃᒻᒥᑉᑐᓂ!

Liitia is excited. But when they get to the hill, she starts to feel nervous. Hunter is a good racer. His one-ski is much nicer than hers, too.

The race is about to start. Hunter counts down.

"Three...two...one...go!" Hunter says.

They speed down the hill. Liitia goes so fast her hat flies off!

ᐊᑯᓂᐆᖕᑎᑐᖅ, ᓖᑎᐊ ᑭᖕᒃᑕᑕᖅᐸᑦᑕᐊᓪᓗᓂ. ᐊᖕᒍᑎᑦᐊᕐᓗᐊᕐᒥ, ᕼᐊᓐᑐᕐ ᓯᒃᑲᑦᓗᐊᖅᑐᐊᓪᓛᓗᓂ.

ᓖᑎᐊ ᑕᑯᓪᓗᓂᐅᒃ ᕼᐊᓐᑐᕐ ᖃᑦᑎᓂᒃᑯᖅᑕᐃᓕᒪᔪᖅ ᐱᙳᕐᒥ. ᓖᑎᐊ ᓴᖕᑦᑕᐅᑎᕐᖕᕐᔪᐊᖅᓗ, ᐊᐳᖅᑐᓂ ᖃᑦᑎᓂᖕᒍᖅ.

Soon Liitia starts to fall behind. She tries to catch up, but Hunter is too fast.

Liitia watches Hunter turn to avoid a bump on the hill. Liitia can't turn fast enough, and she crashes when she hits the bump.

ᕼᐊᓐᑐᕐ ᓴᓚᒃᓴᖅᑐᓂ.

ᓖᑎᐊᒃ ᐊᐳᒪ ᐊᒍᓐᓗᓂᐅᒃ ᓯᐊᓐᔅᐅᑎᒍᐊᑕᓂ. ᐊᓂᓐᒪᕐᑕᖅ, ᑲᖕᒐᑐᐃᓐᓇᖅᑐᖅ.

Hunter wins the race.

Liitia pulls her one-ski out of the snow. She isn't hurt, but she is disappointed.

"ᑕᐃᒻᓐᐊᖅ!" ᓖᑎᐊ ᕼᐊᙳᑐᒥᒃ ᐅᖃᖅᐳᖅ, ᖁᙱᑐᒥ.

ᑕᐃᒻ ᓖᑎᐊ ᐅᔾᔨᖅᑐᓂ ᖃᓂᑐᒦᑦᑐᒥ. ᑕᑯᓪᓗᓂᐅᒃ ᐋᓇᓇᑦᓯᐊᓂ. "ᓱᒪᐃᑦ ᒫᓂ?"
ᐋᓇᓇᑦᓯᐊᖓᑕ ᐃᖅᓱᕐᐊᖅᑐᓂᐅᒃ ᓖᑎᐊ. "ᑕᑯᖃᑕᐅᑦᓴᖅᐸᒃᑲᒥᑦ ᐱᓕᒻᒪᒃᓴᖅᑎᓪᓗᑎᑦ," ᐅᖃᖅᑐᓂ. "ᐅᐱᒋᔭᐅᒋᕐᒃᐱᑦ."

"ᓴᓪᐅᔪᖕᒐ ᑭᒡᐊᓂ!" ᓖᑎᐊ ᐅᖃᖅᐳᖅ. "ᐃᓕᒃᑐᑦ ᓱᒃᓴᖃᐅᑎᕐᓚᐅᖅᓱᒪᔾᔫᒥᕐᑐᖕᒪ."

"Good one!" Liitia says to Hunter, forcing a smile.

Then Liitia notices someone nearby. It is her grandma. "What are you doing here?" Liitia asks.

Grandma gives Liitia a big hug. "I come here to watch you practise sometimes," she says. "I'm proud of you."

"But I lost!" Liitia says. "I'll never be a great racer like you."

ᐊᓈᓇᑦᓯᐊᖕᓗᑕ ᕿᕕᐊᖅᑐᓂᐅᐱ ᓖᑎᐊᒃ ᓯᐊᕐᓂᔭᐅᑎᔭᓕᕐᖕᒪ. ᑎᑯᑦᐊᖅᑐᓂ ᐱᔮᕐᖕᒪᓄᑦ. "ᐅᓇ ᒫᕐᑎᖅᑐᑎᐅᖕᒪᑦ," ᐅᖃᖅᐳᖅ. "ᐱᐊᑎᐊᖅᑐᑦ ᐱᔭᕐᓄᑦ ᓴᒃᓂᖅᓴᐃᑦ. ᒪᓂᖅᑲᖅᓴᑉᑲᖅᑕᕆ."

ᐊᓈᓇᑦᓯᐊᖕᓗᑕ ᓖᑎᐊ ᐅᓂᐊᑉᑎᖕᒪ ᑎᒍᑦᑐᓂᐅᐱ. "ᐊᒃᑐᓇᐅᔭᖅᑎᖅᖃᖅᑐᖕᒪ ᑎᒍᒥᐊᑦ ᐊᔾᔨᔾᓂᐊᕙᖅᑯᑦ," ᐅᖃᖅᐳᖅ. "ᓯᒃᓴᐅᑎᒃᑲᐅᓛᖕᖕᒧᐊᑦ ᓴᓚᐅᕐᖕᒧᖅᑐᑦ ᓯᐊᕐᓂᔭᐅᑎᔭᓕᖕᒫᑦ ᓯᖅᑲᕐᒪᕚᑕ." ᓂᖕᕆᐅᖕᒫ ᖅᑯᖕᓚᕝᖅ.

ᓖᑎᐊ ᐊᑲᐅᓯᕙᓪᓕᐊᓕᒃᑐᓂ.

Grandma looks at Liitia's one-ski. She points to the runner. "This is rusty," she says. "Smooth runners are faster. I can sand this down."

Grandma picks up the pieces of Liitia's handle. "I also have rope to replace your handle," she says. "Even the best racers will lose with a broken one-ski." Grandma smiles.

Liitia starts to feel a bit better.

ᐊᓈᓇᖅᓴᖕᓃᑕ ᓘᑎᐊᓪ ᓴᐊᕐᒃᔭᐅᑐᐊᓕᖕᓂ ᐊᖕᒥᕐᖅᐅᑎᓐᓗᓂᐅᑉ ᐋᖅᑭᑲᕐᕙᕗᑦ. ᐱᑎᑕᐃᓐᓗᓂᐅᑉ, ᐃᖅᑲᐃᑐᖅ. ᐊᑐᕐᓇᖃᒻᒥᓂ ᓴᒨᔮᕐᒥᓂ ᑕᑯᔭᖅ ᓴᐊᕐᒃᔭᐅᑐᐊᓪᑎᐊᔪᓛᐅᔭᑦᒃᒥ. ᓘᑎᐊ ᓴᖕᓇᑎᖕᓴᕋᓯᖅᑲ ᐱᐅᓂᖅᒐᒥᒃ ᓴᐊᕐᒃᔭᐅᑐᐊᓚᖕᒥ ᓂᑎᐅᖕᕋᓱᖅᓕᓪᓗᓂᐅᑉ ᓴᓇᖅᕙᕋᓯᖅᕙᑕ.

ᓴᐊᕐᒃᔭᐅᑐᐊᓚᒃ ᐱᓇᓱᐊᖅᓯᒃᓯᕐᓱᖕᓂ ᓴᓇᒨᓂᐅᑉ.

Grandma takes Liitia's one-ski home and fixes it. As she is working, she has an idea. She sees some materials in her shed that would make a nice one-ski. She decides to make Liitia a better one-ski and surprise her at the competition.

She works on the new one-ski over the next few weeks.

ᐊᓇᓇᓯᐊᖕᒥᑦ ᓴᓂᔭᓐᖓᒍ ᓯᑎᐊᖕ ᓯᐊᕐᓯᐅᑎᒐᓕᕐᖕᒪ, ᒪᐅᓯᓂᖃᖕᔭᖕᓕᖅᑐᓂ. ᓯᑎᐊ ᒪᓕᒪᒃᐊᖕᓇᖕᖃᖅᑐᖅ ᓴᓇᖃᕆᖅᑐᖃᓐᓇᐅᖕᒪᓂᖕ. ᓯᖃᐅᑎᖃᑎᖃᖕᖃᖅᑐᓂ ᐃᐊᖕᔪᒃ ᐊᔪᖕᕐᖕᓇᔪ ᓯᑭᓯᖕᒃ. ᓯᓐ ᓴᖃᑎᔪᓇ ᒪᒃᐅᑎᕐᓇᓂ. ᓴᖕᔪᒌᐊᖃᖅᑯᖕᔪᓕᕐᖅᑐᓂ.

ᑎᓯᖕᖕᓇᖅ ᐃᓯᓕᓐᖅᑎᓐᒎᒍ, ᓴᓐᖃᖃᕐᓯᖕᓇᖅ ᑎᑭᕝᓛᖅ. ᖃᐅᓯᐃᑐᖕᒌᓚᓕᖕ ᑕᑯᖕᓇᐊᖅᑐᑎᖕ ᓯᖃᐅᑎᓂᐊᖅᑐᓂᖕ.

After Grandma fixes up Liitia's old one-ski, it works a bit better. Liitia keeps practising until the competition. She does more races with Hunter and the other kids. She's still not as good as them, but she gets better and better. She becomes really good at going around corners.

The end of the season comes, and soon it is the day of the competition. Almost everyone in Qausuittuq comes to watch the races.

ᓖᑎᐊᑉ ᐊᓈᓇᑦᓯᐊᓂ ᑕᑯᓗᓂᐅᒃ ᐃᓄᒐᓱᖕᑐᖅ. ᑎᒍᒥᐊᖅᑐᓂ ᓴᐊᖕᓴᐅᑎᔪᐊᓚᑎᐊᕚᓪᓗᖕᒥᒃ ᓄᑖᒥᒃ! ᐃᒃᓯᕙᐅᑦᑎᐊᕐᓂᒃᑐᓂ ᐱᔾᔫᒥᓪᓗ ᒪᓂᕋᑎᐊᖅᑐᒥᒃ.

Liitia finds her grandma in the crowd. She is holding a beautiful new one-ski! It has a nice seat and a smooth runner.

"ᓴᓇᐅᖅᑕᕋ ᐃᓐᖕᓄᑦ," ᐊᓈᓇᑦᓯᐊᖓ ᐅᖃᖅᐳᖅ. "ᒪᖕᒥᐊᓗᖕᒥᒃ
ᑎᒌᕋᐅᑎᒥᒃ ᐱᐅᓂᖅᓴᒥᒃ ᐱᖃᕐᐊᖃᕋᕕᑦ."

"I made it for you," Grandma says. "You need something better than that old rusty sled."

ᓖᑎᐊ ᑕᐸᐃᖅᐳᖅ. "ᐅᒃᐱᕆᔫᖕᒥᑦᑐᖕᒐ."
ᐅᖃᖅᐳᖅ. "ᖁᔭᓐᓇᒦᒃ, ᖁᔭᓐᓇᒦᒃ,
ᖁᔭᓐᓇᒦᒃ!"

"ᑕᐃᒪᓗᐊᖅ," ᐊᓈᓇᑦᓯᐊᖓ ᐅᖃᖅᐳᖅ.
"ᓱᒃᑲᔪᐅᑎᓱᓐᐊᖅᑲᕋᕕᑦ!"

Liitia is shocked. "I can't believe it!" she says. "Thank you, thank you, thank you!"

"Enough of all that," says Grandma. "You have a race to do!"

ᓯᕗᓪᓕᖅᐹᖅ ᓯᒃᑲᓴᐅᑕᐅᔪᖅ ᐳᒃᓴᓂᖅ. ᓯᒪᔮᑦ ᐊᔪᙱᕆᓂᖅᓴᐃᑦ ᑕᐃᒪᐃᓕᐅᖅᑐᓄᑦ ᐃᓚᐅᓕᕐᔪᑎᒃ. ᓖᑎᐊ ᑕᑯᓐᓇᖅᑐᓂ ᐳᒃᖅᑎᓪᓗᒋᑦ. ᓂᑎᐅᒃᑭᖅ ᑕᐃᒪᐃᓕᐅᖃᑕᐅᖃᑦᑖᕐᓯᓂᕐᒥᓂᒃ.

The first race is the ski jump. The experienced older kids compete in that race. Liitia watches them go over the big jumps. She hopes she can do that someday.

ᕼᐊᓐᑐᕐ ᓴᓚᒋᔪᓂᕐᑦ ᑕᐃᒪᐃᓕᐅᖅᑐᑦ. ᖁᕕᐊᕈᓐᓴᓂᐅᖅ. ᖃᐅᔨᒪᒻᒪᒍ ᐱᓕᒻᒪᒃᓴᖃᑦᑕᓂᕐᒪᓂᒃ.

ᑕᐃᕙᓂ ᓖᑎᐊ ᓯᒃᑲᓴᐅᑎᓂᐊᕐᓂᖓ ᐱᒋᐊᖅᐳᖅ - ᓴᕿᐊᓇᖅᑐᒃᑯᑦ. ᑕᐃᕙᓂ ᓯᒃᓂᒃᑲᐅᑎᓂᕐᒥ, ᐱᖅᑕᐅᔪᑦ ᓴᕿᒃᑕᓚᒃᑕᕆᐊᖃᖅᑐᑦ.

Hunter wins that race. She cheers for him. She knows how much he's been practising.

Now it is time for Liitia's race—the slalom. In this race, people have to go around a lot of sharp corners.

ᓖᑎᐊ ᓱᖁᓴᓪᓗᓂ ᐱᒋᐊᑐᐃᓐᓇᕆᐊᖃᓕᖅᐳᖅ ᐱᖁᒃ ᖃᖕᒥᓂ. ᓯᒃᑲᓯᓂᖅ ᐱᒋᐊᖅᐳᖅ.

Liitia is nervous as she gets into position at the top of the hill. Then the race starts.

ᓯᐊᕐᓯᐅᑐᐊᓚᖅᑕᖃᐅᒥᓄᑦ,
ᓕᑎᐊ ᓱᑲᓂᖅᓴᓕᓂᐊᔪᑉᖅ
ᓱᑲᓕᖃᖅᒍᐊᑕᒥᓂᒃ! ᑎᓂᖅᑯᑖᒪᓕᒃᑯᖅᑐᓂ,
ᐊᐅᓚᑦᑎᑦᑎᐊᖅᑐᓂ ᓱᑲᑦᑎᐊᖅᑐᓂᓗ. ᑕᕝᕙᑦ
ᓕᑎᐊ ᓯᕗᓪᓕᖅᐸᐅᖅᑐᓂ.

ᓕᑎᐊ ᓴᓚᖅᖅᐳᖅ!

On her new one-ski, Liitia starts going faster than she ever has before! She makes it around all the corners, feeling completely in control and keeping a good speed. Soon Liitia pulls into the lead.

Liitia wins!

ᓖᑎᐊᑉ ᐊᓈᓇᑦᓯᐊᓂ ᑕᑯᓪᓗᓂᐅᒃ ᖁᕕᐊᑦᓱᖅ ᐃᓄᒌᐊᓂ. ᐱᒃᑯᒥᓈᕐᓗᓂ ᓱᒃᑲᖃᐅᑎᓭᒥ ᐊᓈᓇᑦᓯᐊᕐᒥᔫᑦ.

ᐊᑕᐅᓯᒃᑲᓂᕐᒥᒃ ᓱᒃᑲᐅᑎᓂᖃᖅᓯᓂᐊᕐᒪᑕ ᐅᓪᓗᒥ - ᐃᓐᓇᐃᑦ ᓱᒃᑲᓯᓂᖕᒥᑕ. ᓖᑎᐊᑉ ᐊᓈᓇᑦᓯᐊᓂ ᑕᑯᓐᓇᒋᒥᔾᔪᓂᐅᖅ, ᓇᓂᔭᓐᓇᖏᒥᓱ.

ᐅᖃᖅᐸᓪᓚᑏᐳ ᓈᓴᐃᖅᑎᓪᓗᒍ, ᓖᑎᐊᑉ ᑕᑯᕚ ᐊᓈᓇᑦᓯᐊᓂ ᐱᖕᔫᑉ ᖃᖕᓕᓂ. ᓖᑎᐊᑉ ᓯᐊᕐᓯᔪᐅᑎᔪᐊᓕᖅᖕᓕᓂᒃ ᐊᑐᖅᑐᖅ. ᓱᒃᑲᓴᓯᒃᑐᖅ!

Liitia sees her grandma cheering in the crowd. She is proud to be a great racer like her grandma.

There is one more race today—the Elders' race. Liitia wants to watch it with her grandma, but she can't find her.

The announcer counts down, and Liitia sees her grandma at the top of the hill. She has Liitia's old one-ski. She is going to race!

ᓄᒃᓯᐅᑎᓂᖅ ᐱᒋᐊᖅᑐᓂ, ᐋᓇᓇᑦᓯᐊᖕᒪ
ᓯᕗᓪᓕᐅᖅᑐᖅᑐᓂ. ᓯᐊᕐᓯᐅᑎᑐᐊᓕᑐᖅᑲᕈᓐᓗᒃ,
ᓄᒃᑕᕐᐊᔪᕐᓚᒃ ᓕᑎᐊᑉ ᐊᖓᒻᒪᑎᔅᓇᑦᐊᖕᒧᓕᓃᒃᑕᖕᓗ!
ᐋᓇᓇᑦᓯᐊᖕᒪ ᓄᒃᓯᐅᑎᒃᐅᓯᓕᓴᑎᐊᓗᒃ.

ᓕᑎᐊᑉ ᐋᓇᓇᑦᓯᐊᖕᒪ ᓯᕗᓕᓕᖅᐸᒃᒧᖕᓗᓂ ᓴᓕᖅᖅᑐᓂ,
ᓕᑎᐊ ᓂᐱᖅᑯᖅᑐᓕᑎᐊᒧᖕᓗᓂ ᖁᕕᐊᓕᕐᖅ.

The race starts, and Grandma is instantly in the lead. Even with the old one-ski, she is so fast that Liitia can barely keep track of her! Grandma truly is the best racer around.

Liitia's grandma wins first place, and Liitia cheers louder than anybody else.

ᓵᓚᖅᑲᕋᓱᖕᓂᖅ ᐃᓱᓕᒃᑐᓂ, ᓵᓚᖅᑲᖅᑐᑦᑐ ᓵᓚᖅᑲᐅᓯᐊᖅᑐᖅᑐᑎᒃ. ᓖᑎᐊ ᓵᓚᖅᑲᐅᓯᐊᖅᑐᓂ ᕿᓲᖕᓂᒃ ᐳᐊᓘᖕᓂᒃ. ᐊᓈᓇᑦᓯᐊᖓ ᕿᓯᖕᒥ ᓵᓚᖅᑲᐅᓯᐊᖅᑐᓂ.

“ᑭᖑᓪᓕᖅᒥᖅᑲᐃ ᑖᓐᓇ ᐊᑐᖖᓛᓕᖅᑕᕋ!” ᐊᓈᓇᑦᓯᐊᖓ ᐅᖃᖅᐳᖅ, ᑎᒍᒥᐊᖅᑐᓂ ᕿᓯᖕᒥ.

ᐊᓈᓇᑦᓯᐊᖓ ᓖᑎᐊᓗ ᐃᒡᓚᖅᐴᒃ. ᓖᑎᐊᑉ ᑎᒍᓪᓗᓂᒋᒃ ᐳᐊᓗᑖᖅᑲᐅᖕᓂᒃ ᓯᐊᕐᓇᔭᐅᑎᑐᐊᓕᑖᖅᑲᐅᓂᓗ. ᐅᑭᐅᖅ ᖁᕕᐊᓇᖅᑐᐊᓘᖅᑲᐅᔪᖅ. ᓖᑎᐊ ᐊᑯᓂᒍᓱᐊᑦᑐᓂ ᓯᐊᕐᓇᔭᐅᑎᑐᐊᓕᓂ ᐅᑭᐅᖑᓛᖅᑐᖅ ᐊᑐᓛᕋᒥᐅᒃ!

The competition ends, and the winners collect their prizes. Liitia wins a pair of sealskin mitts. Grandma wins a sealskin.

"Maybe I'll race on this next time!" says Grandma, holding up the sealskin.

Grandma and Liitia laugh. Liitia picks up her new mitts and her new one-ski. This spring has been so much fun. Liitia can't wait to race on her one-ski again next year!